Marine Corps Historical Publications Catalog

*Available Publications List
and Chronological Bibliography*

Henry I. Shaw, Jr.
Compiler

History and Museums Division
Headquarters, U.S. Marine Corps
Washington, D.C.
1988

Table of Contents

Introduction

Since 1920 the historians of the United States Marine Corps have produced several hundred works on Marine Corps history. These have ranged in length from a few pages of mimeographed material to lengthy case-bound histories sold by the Government Printing Office (GPO) through the Superintendent of Documents. This catalog is in two parts. The first lists those publications still in print and available from the Superintendent of Documents (in which case the GPO stock number and price is given) or only from the History and Museums Division (in which case the abbreviation MCH&M is included). Most of the historical works sold by the GPO are available free to recognized libraries and similar institutions on request to the History and Museums Division. Many of the publications marked MCH&M are intended for limited distribution, and are not generally available to individuals. This is particularly true of Occasional Papers which are reproductions of original copy from various sources. These have the additional marking of an asterisk, i.e., MCH&M*.

The second part of the catalog is a chronological list of all significant historical publications that were officially produced or sponsored by the History and Museums Division and its predecessors. There are a host also of historical briefs which are not listed. These were produced, mainly by the historians of the Reference Section, in answer to repetitive questions on popular subjects. These are regularly revised and updated and are not generally considered in the class of publications.

Operational and administrative histories of the Marine Corps are listed in chronological order under the "General Histories" section of this catalog. Most of the monographs and casebound histories which were published concerning World War II and Korean War campaigns are long out of print, but possibly may be obtained from booksellers who stock or are willing to search for earlier Marine Corps histories. A list of such booksellers is maintained by the division and may be obtained on request.

The division is currently engaged in writing a nine-volume chronological history of Marine Corps operations in Vietnam, the first five volumes of which are listed in this catalog. Well along toward completion is a series of histories of the active duty and Reserve infantry and artillery regiments of the Corps. A similar series of squadron histories is an on-going project. The first modern-day history of a major Marine Corps base, Quantico, has been published and more base histories are planned or underway. An ambitious overall history of the Corps has been started with a history of Marines in the Revolution and similar histories of significant eras are planned or in preparation.

Fortitudine, the bulletin of the Marine Corps Historical Program, is published quarterly and distributed throughout the Corps.

GPO publications may be obtained by writing to:

Superintendent of Documents
Government Printing Office
Washington, D.C. 20402

(Be sure to include stock number and check or money order with each order.)

Publications of the History and Museums Division, under the conditions outlined above, may be obtained by writing to:

Marine Corps Historical Center (Code HDS-1)
Building 58, Washington Navy Yard
Washington, D.C. 20374-0580

Part I Available Publications

General Histories

Uniforms of the American Marines, 1775 to 1829. Maj Edwin N. McClellan, USMC. 1932. 1974 reprint. 99 pages. 21 illustrations. Reproduction of the original monograph with contemporary illustrations. *MCH&M.*

A Brief History of U.S. Marine Corps Officer Procurement, 1775-1969. Bernard C. Nalty and LtCol Ralph F. Moody, USMC. 1970 rev. ed. Outlines the process and problems of officer procurement throughout the history of the Marine Corps. Soft cover. *MCH&M.*

A Brief History of Headquarters Marine Corps Staff Organization. Kenneth W. Condit, *et al.* 1970 rev. ed. 49 pages. 7 sketches. Concise account of the evolution of Marine Corps staff organization. Soft cover. *MCH&M.*

United States Marine Corps Ranks and Grades, 1775-1969. Bernard C. Nalty, *et al.* 1970. 62 pages. 1 sketch. 20 photographs. Appendices. Historical survey of the development of officer and enlisted ranks and grades. Soft cover. *MCH&M.*

Marines in the Revolution: A History of the Continental Marines in the American Revolution, 1775-1783. Charles R. Smith. 500 pages. 14 original color paintings by Maj Charles Waterhouse, USMCR. 245 illustrations. 4 maps. 25 photographs. Appendices. Detailed account of Continental Marine actions during the Revolution based on contemporary sources, including several diaries and journals. Hard cover. *MCH&M.*

Pictorial History of the Marines in the Revolution. 1975. 32 pages. Black and white reproductions of the 14 paintings by Major Charles Waterhouse, USMCR, with summary descriptions. Soft cover. *MCH&M.*

Marines in the Frigate Navy, 1798-1835. Col Charles H. Waterhouse, USMCR, artist and Charles R. Smith. 1985. 14 color plates and 17 pages of text. Depicts historic incidents in the history of the Corps in the day of sail. Glossy plates and soft cover. *MCH&M.*

1

One Hundred and Eighty Landings of United States Marines, 1800-1934. Capt Harry A. Ellsworth, USMC. 1934. 1975 reprint. 163 pages. Brief descriptions of amphibious operations by Marines. Soft cover. *MCH&M*.

The Eagle, Globe and Anchor, 1858-1969. Col John A. Driscoll, USMCR. 1971. 1977 reprint. 164 pages. 136 illustrations. Appendices. Traces history of the Marine Corps emblem and its various uses on the uniform. Soft cover. *MCH&M*.

United States Marines at Harpers Ferry and in the Civil War. Bernard C. Nalty. 1966 rev. ed. 26 pages. 1 map. Short narrative of Marine Corps participation in the events at Harpers Ferry federal armory and in the actions of the War Between the States. Includes battle at Drewry's Bluff where Cpl John Mackie, first Marine to receive Medal of Honor, was engaged. Soft cover. *MCH&M*.

Civil War Marine, A Diary of the Red River Expedition, 1864. Frank L. Church. Edited and annotated by James P. Jones and Edward F. Keuchel. 1975. 89 pages. 19 illustrations. Personal journal of Civil War Marine officer serving on board ship in this expedition. Soft cover. *MCH&M*.

The United States Marines in the War with Spain. Bernard C. Nalty. 1967 rev. ed. 20 pages. Short general account of the War of 1898. Battles include Manila and Guantanamo. Soft cover. *MCH&M*.

Progress and Purpose: A Developmental History of the United States Marine Corps, 1900-1970. LtCol Kenneth J. Clifford, USMCR. 1973. 156 pages. 6 maps and sketches. 83 photographs. Appendices. Index. The development of doctrine, tactics, and techniques of amphibious warfare from the Advanced Base Force to V/STOL. Includes an outline of the development of the Landing Operations Manual. Soft cover. *MCH&M*.

The United States Marines in Nicaragua. Bernard C. Nalty. 1961 rev. ed. 1968 reprint. 39 pages. 2 maps. Role of Marine Corps in the American interventions in Nicaragua, 1910-1933. Soft cover. *MCH&M*.

Marines in the Dominican Republic, 1916-1924. Capt Stephen M. Fuller, USMCR, and Graham A. Cosmas. 1974.

109 pages. 65 illustrations, including appendix of 35 photographs from album of BGen Robert H. Dunlap, USMC. Account of Marine Corps presence in the Dominican Republic based on official reports, memoirs, personal correspondence, and recollections of participants. Soft cover. *MCH&M.*

The United States Marine Corps in the World War. Maj Edwin N. McClellan, USMC. 1920. 1968 reprint. 109 pages. 1 photograph. Appendix. Index. Accurate, useful, and concise accounting of the growth, activities, and combat exploits of Marines in 1917-1918. Belleau Wood, Aisne-Marne. Soft cover. *MCH&M.*

Marine Flyer in France, The Diary of Captain Alfred A. Cunningham, November 1917-January 1918. Capt Alfred A. Cunningham, USMC. Edited by Graham A. Cosmas. 1974. 43 pages. 8 photographs. Experiences and personal impressions of the first Marine aviator when he toured British and French aviation facilities during World War I. Soft cover. *MCH&M.*

Women Marines in World War I. Capt Linda L. Hewitt, USMCR. 1974. 65 pages. 30 photographs. Appendices. Account of women Marines' service based largely on veterans' accounts. Soft cover. *MCH&M.*

Quantico: Crossroads of the Marine Corps. LtCol Charles A. Fleming, USMC, Capt Robin L. Austin, USMC, and Capt Charles A. Braley III, USMC. 1978. 146 pages. 83 photographs. 4 maps. Appendices. Index. A history of the Marine Corps base and its immediate area from the 1600s to the present day, when it is the principal officer training command in the Marine Corps. Soft cover. Hardcover edition available for library distribution. *MCH&M.*

The United States Marines in Iceland, 1941-1942. LtCol Kenneth J. Clifford, USMCR. 1970. 22 pages. 1 map. 1 photograph. Appendix. Bibliography. Briefly describes the background and reasons for the Marine move to the island. Illustrates a force in readiness. Soft cover. *MCH&M.*

The United States Marines in the Guadalcanal Campaign. Henry I. Shaw, Jr. 1962 rev. ed. 1969 reprint. 14 pages. Bibliography. Concise account of the 1st and 2d Marine Division's operations, 7 August 1942-8 February 1943. Soft cover. *MCH&M.*

***The United States Marines on Iwo Jima: The Battle and
the Flag-Raising***. Bernard C. Nalty. 1967. 1970 reprint. 29
pages. 1 map. 9 photographs. Appendix. A concise narrative
of the battle and the events leading to the famous flag raising. Individual biographies of those involved in the flag raising. Soft cover. *MCH&M*.

***History of U.S. Marine Corps Operations in World War
II: Western Pacific Operations***. George W. Garand and Truman R. Strobridge. 848 pages. 42 maps and charts. 58 photographs. Appendices. Index. Details the evolution of FMFPac,
combat on Peleliu, air support in the western pacific, and the
campaign on Iwo Jima, largest all-Marine operation in World
War II. Hard cover. *MCH&M*. Available for library distribution.

***History of U.S. Marine Corps Operations in World War
II: Victory and Occupation***. Benis M. Frank and Henry I.
Shaw, Jr. 945 pages. 47 maps. 64 photographs. Appendices.
Index. Describes the last major combat operation of World
War II on Okinawa and postwar occupation activities in the
Pacific Islands, in Japan, and in North China. Summarizes
the Marine Corps contribution to the war. Hard cover.
MCH&M. Available for library distribution.

***United States Marine Corps Special Units of World War
II***. Charles L. Updegraph, Jr. 1972. 1977 reprint. 105 pages.
11 maps. 17 photographs. Appendices. A brief narrative of
experimental special purpose units organized by the Marine
Corps for World War II, including raider, parachute, and
defense battalions, and barrage balloon and glider squadrons.
Soft cover. *MCH&M*.

Blacks in the Marine Corps. Henry I. Shaw, Jr., and Ralph
W. Donnelly. 1975. 1988 reprint. 109 pages. 5 maps. 2 charts.
40 photographs. Appendices. Index. A concise account of the
service of black Marines from 1942-1973 with special empha-
sis on the black units of World War II. Includes photographs
and citations of all black Marine Medal of Honor recipients.
Soft cover. *MCH&M*.

Marine Corps Women's Reserve in World War II. LtCol
Pat Meid, USMCR. 1968 rev. ed. 98 pages. Appendices. General history of women in the Marine Corps from February 1943
through demobilization. Soft cover. *MCH&M*.

The United States Marines in the Occupation of Japan.
Henry I. Shaw, Jr. 1962 rev. ed. 1969 reprint. 29 pages. 2 maps.
Concise narrative of major events that took place when Marine units deployed to Japan at close of World War II. Includes operations of 4th Marines and MAG-31 at Yokosuka and 2d and 5th Marine Divisions with MAG-22 in Kyushu and Honshu. Soft cover. *MCH&M.*

The United States Marines in North China, 1945-1949.
Henry I. Shaw, Jr. 1962 rev. ed. 1968 reprint. 33 pages. 2 maps.
Appendices. Operations of 1st and 6th Marine Divisions and the 1st Marine Aircraft Wing in Hopeh and Shantung Provinces, China. Deactivation of the 6th Marine Division and formation of Fleet Marine Force, Western Pacific. Soft cover. *MCH&M.*

Marines and Helicopters, 1946-1962. LtCol Eugene W. Rawlins, USMC. Edited by Maj William J. Sambito, USMC. 1976. 113 pages. 15 charts and tables. 36 photographs. Appendices. Index. A developmental history of the procurement and employment of helicopters by the Marine Corps in the early years of the emergence of the doctrine of vertical envelopment. Soft cover. *MCH&M.*

A History of the Woman Marines, 1946-1977. Col Mary V. Stremlow, USMCR. 250 pages. 128 photographs. Appendices. Index. Covers the integration of women into the regular Marine Corps through the dissolution of separate WM units and abolition of director's office. Chapters on training, administration, promotions, marriage and motherhood, uniforms, traditions. Soft cover. *MCH&M.* Hard-cover edition available for library distribution.

Mobilization of the Marine Corps Reserve in the Korean Conflict, 1950-1951. Capt Ernest H. Giusti, USMCR. 1950. 1967 reprint. 80 pages. 20 charts. Analysis of the administrative aspects of subject through June 1951. Illustrates importance of strong Reserve. Soft cover. *MCH&M.*

Operations in West Korea: U.S. Marine Operations in Korea, 1950-1953, Vol. V. LtCol Pat Meid, USMCR, and Maj James M. Yingling, USMC. 1972. 643 pages. 35 maps and sketches. 71 photographs. Appendices. Index. 1st Marine Division and 1st Marine Aircraft Wing in Korea from March 1952 through end of war in defense of corridor to Seoul on western end of I Corps front. Battles include Bunker Hill,

Hook, Nevadas, Boulder City. Hard cover. *MCH&M*. Available for library distribution.

Marines in Lebanon, 1958. Jack Shulimson. 1966. 1983 rev. ed. 50 pages. 3 maps. 3 photographs. Appendices. Shows the Marine Corps role in carrying out American foreign policy during the Lebanon crisis in 1958. Illustrates show of force. Soft cover. *MCH&M*.

The Marines in Vietnam 1954-1973: An Anthology and Annotated Bibiography. 1974. 1983 reprint. 1985 rev. ed. 373 pages. 51 maps and sketches. 177 photographs. Articles from *Marine Corps Gazette, U.S. Naval Institute Proceedings*, and *Naval Review* concerning Marine Corps activities in Vietnam through 1975 and a bibliography of related articles from the same publications. Soft cover. GPO 008-055-00168-4. $22.00. Available for library distribution.

Marines and Helicopters, 1962-1973. LtCol Williams R. Fails, USMC. 1978. 251 pages. 5 charts. 67 photographs. Appendices. Index. Continues the story of the procurement and employment of helicopters in the Marine Corps. Soft cover. GPO 008-055-00112-9. $8.50. Hard cover edition available for library distribution.

U.S. Marines in Vietnam: The Advisory and Combat Assistance Era, 1954-1964. Capt Robert H. Whitlow, USMCR. 1977. 1982 reprint. 190 pages. 22 maps and charts. 37 photographs. Appendices. Index. An accounting of the Marine advisory effort and buildup of the Vietnamese Marine Corps prior to the introduction of major U.S. ground combat units to South Vietnam. Details as well the Marine helicopter assistance to the South Vietnamese armed forces from 1962-1964. Soft cover. GPO 008-055-00094-7. $11.00. Hard cover edition available for library distribution.

Chaplains with Marines in Vietnam, 1962-1971. Cdr Herbert L. Bergsma, CHC, USN. 1985. 240 pages. 1 map. 72 photographs. Story of Navy chaplains' service with Marine units within the overall framework of Vietnam operations. Lists all Navy chaplains who served in III MAF. Highlights the accomplishments of representative junior and senior chaplains. Soft cover. Hard cover edition available for library distribution. *MCH&M*

U.S. Marine Corps Civic Action Effort in Vietnam, March 1965-March 1966. Capt Russell H. Stolfi, USMCR. 1968. 96

pages. 5 maps and sketches. 23 photographs. Appendix. Story of first formative year of III Marine Amphibious Force civilian aid. County Fair, Golden Fleece, and Combined Action programs. Soft cover. *MCH&M.*

U.S. Marines in Vietnam: The Landing and the Buildup, 1965. Jack Shulimson and Maj Charles M. Johnson, USMC. 1978. 260 pages. 121 photographs. 17 maps. Appendices. Index. The full story of the first year of the commitment of Marine ground combat and air units to the Vietnam War, including the operations of special landing forces and advisors. Soft cover. GPO 008-055-00129-3. $8.00. Hard-cover edition available for library distribution.

U.S. Marines in Vietnam: An Expanding War, 1966. Jack Shulimson. 1982. 390 pages. 37 maps. 192 photographs. Appendices. Index. Adding the 1st Marine Division to III MAF and activation of Force Logistic Command to support increasing combat operations. The Vietnamese political crisis in the spring and the movement of Marine units north to engage North Vietnamese regular units. Soft cover. *MCH&M.* Hard cover edition available for library distribution.

U.S. Marine Corps Civil Affairs in I Corps, Republic of South Vietnam, April 1966-April 1967. Capt William D. Parker, USMCR. 1970. 131 pages. 2 maps and sketches. 7 photographs. Appendices. Describes the continued growth of the III Marine Amphibious Force's civic action program. Soft cover. *MCH&M.*

Small Unit Action in Vietnam, Summer 1966. Capt Francis J. West, Jr., USMCR. 1967. 1977 reprint. 123 pages. 7 maps and sketches. 13 photographs. Appendix. Short, factual narratives of small unit engagements, including graphic description of action for which SSgt Jimmie E. Howard received the Medal of Honor. Soft cover. GPO 008-055-00115-3. $6.50. Available for library distribution.

U.S. Marines in Vietnam: Fighting the North Vietnamese, 1967. Maj Gary L. Telfer, USMC, LtCol Lane Rogers, USMC, and V. Keith Fleming, Jr. 1984. 338 pages. 21 maps. 197 photographs. Appendices. Index. Focuses on the change of thrust of III MAF operations to northern I Corps and the DMZ. Introduction of U.S. Army reinforcements in the south.

Extensive pacification operations by the CAPs. Soft cover. GPO 008-055-00165-0. $10.00. Hard cover edition available for library distribution.

The Battle of Khe Sanh. Capt Moyers S. Shore II, USMC. 1969. 1977 reprint. 203 pages. 10 maps and sketches. 42 photographs. Appendices. The stand of the 26th Marines at the Khe Sanh Combat Base and airstrip. The importance of supporting arms and sound logistics. April 1967-June 1968. Some David D. Duncan photos. Soft cover. GPO 008-055-00114-5. $7.00. Available for library distribution.

U.S. Marines in Vietnam: Vietnamization and Redeployment, 1970-1971. Graham A. Cosmas and LtCol Terrence P. Murray, USMC. Maj William R. Melton, USMC, and Jack Shulimson, editors. 487 pages. 12 maps. 167 photographs. Appendices. Index. 1986. Covers the gradual withdrawal of Marine combat forces from Vietnam and the concentration of Marine activities in Quang Nam Province. The assumption of area command by the Army's XXIV Corps and the phasedown of III MAF to 3d MAB. Troubles over race and drugs in rear areas. Soft cover. GPO 008-005-00169-2. $29.00. Hard cover edition available for library distribution.

U.S. Marine Corps Uniforms, 1983. Capt Donna J. Neary, USMCR, artist, and Capt Steven M. Berkowitz, USMC. 12 plates and 13-page description. Detailed and extremely accurate depictions of the full range of officer and enlisted uniforms and insignia in 1983. Glossy paper reproduction and soft cover. *MCH&M.*

U.S. Marines in Grenada, 1983. LtCol Ronald H. Spector, USMCR. 1987. 35 pages. 4 maps. 10 photographs and illustrations. Appendices. Description of Marine Amphibious Unit 22's operations in the capture of the island. Soft cover. GPO 008-055-00170-6. $2.75. Available for library distribution.

U.S. Marines in Lebanon, 1982-1984. Benis M. Frank. 1987. 4 maps. 135 photographs and illustrations. Appendices. Index. Relates the activities of Marine units in the Lebanon peacekeeping effort, including the tragic October 1983 bombing of the BLT barracks and its aftermath. Soft cover. GPO 008-055-0171-4. $10.00. Available for library distribution.

Unit Histories

The 1st Marine Division and Its Regiments. 1974. 24 pages. 20 photographs. Includes World War II action at Guadalcanal, Cape Gloucester, Peleliu, and Okinawa; Korean War; Vietnam. Soft cover. *MCH&M*.

The 2d Marine Division and Its Regiments. 1984. 56 pages. 36 photographs. Includes World War I activities and World War II actions at Guadalcanal, Tarawa, Saipan, Tinian, and Okinawa; Lebanon 1958 and 1982-84; Cuba 1962; and Grenada 1983. Soft cover. *MCH&M*.

The 3d Marine Division and Its Regiments. 1975. 25 pages. 25 photographs. Includes short histories and lineage and honors of the division and its four line regiments. A supplement covering the 21st and 26th Marines is included. Soft cover. *MCH&M*.

A Brief History of the 1st Marines. Maj John H. Johnstone, USMC. 1968 rev. ed. 46 pages. Appendices. Traces 1st Marines history from 1899 to 1967. Details on early interventions. Soft cover. *MCH&M*.

A Brief History of the 2d Marines. Capt Robert J. Kane, USMC. 1969 rev. ed. 58 pages. 6 maps. 11 photographs. Appendices. From 1901 to 1969. Antibandit operations in Caribbean. World War II includes Guadalcanal, Tarawa, Saipan, and occupation of Kyushu. Soft cover. *MCH&M*.

A Brief History of the 3d Marines. Benis M. Frank. 1968 rev. ed. 47 pages. 2 maps. Appendices. From 1911 to 1966. Dominican Republic campaign 1916-1920. World War II includes Bougainville, Guam, and North China. Vietnam. Soft cover. *MCH&M*.

A Brief History of the 4th Marines. James S. Santelli. 1970. 68 pages. 6 maps. 14 photographs. Appendices. From 1914 to 1969. Mexican and Caribbean campaigns. Pre-World War II duty in China. Fall of Corregidor. Landings on Guam, Okinawa, and Japan. Vietnam. Soft cover. *MCH&M*.

A Brief History of the 6th Marines. LtGen William K. Jones, USMC (Ret). 1987. 181 pages. 9 maps. 92 photographs. Appendices. 1917-1986. World War I; China; Iceland. World

War II campaigns on Guadalcanal, Tarawa, Saipan, and Tinian. Japan occupation. Lebanon; Cuba; Dominican Republic. Soft cover. GPO 008-055-00177-2. $11.00. Available for library distribution.

A Brief History of the 7th Marines. James S. Santelli. 1980. 84 pages. 9 maps. 60 photographs. Appendices. 1917-1978. Intervention in Cuba. World War II campaigns on Guadalcanal, Cape Gloucester, Peleliu, and Okinawa; North China; Korea; Vietnam. Soft cover. *MCH&M.*

A Brief History of the 8th Marines. James S. Santelli. 1976. 103 pages. 8 maps. 28 photographs. Appendices. Raised in 1917, the regiment served in Texas and Haiti and was disbanded in 1925. Reactivated in World War II, it served on Guadalcanal, Tarawa, Saipan, Tinian, and Okinawa. Subsequent service included Lebanon, Cuban missile crisis, and Dominican Republic. Soft cover. *MCH&M.*

A Brief History of the 10th Marines. Maj David N. Buckner, USMC. 1981. 131 pages. 9 maps. 80 photographs. Appendices. 1914-1981. Vera Cruz, Haiti, and Dominican Republic. Mail guard, China, Iceland, Samoa. World War II battles for Guadalcanal, Tarawa, Saipan, Tinian, Okinawa. Japan, Lebanon, Cuba. Soft cover. *MCH&M.*

A Brief History of the 12th Marines. Charles R. Smith. 1972. 84 pages. 5 maps. 13 photographs. The 12th Marines in World War II including Bougainville, Guam, Iwo Jima. The postwar years, the cold war period, and Vietnam. Also furnishes a general history of the development of Marine Corps artillery. Soft cover. *MCH&M.*

A Brief History of the 25th Marines. Col Joseph B. Ruth, Jr., USMCR. 1981. 60 pages. 4 maps. 28 photographs. Appendices. 1943-1977. World War II campaigns of Marshalls, Marianas, and Iwo Jima. Reserve service from 1962 of eastern and midwest units. Soft cover. *MCH&M.*

A History of Marine Observation Squadron Six. LtCol Gary W. Parker, USMC, and Maj Frank M. Batha, USMC. 1982. 73 pages. 6 maps. 56 photographs. 1920-1977. Wide variety of experience and aircraft in Nicaragua, Okinawa, Korea (first combat use of helicopters), and Vietnam. Soft cover. *MCH&M.*

A History of Marine Medium Helicopter Squadron 161. LtCol Gary W. Parker, USMC. 1978. 47 pages. 24 photographs. Appendices. A concise account of the Marine Corps' first transport helicopter squadron with highlights of its service in Korea, Hawaii, Vietnam, and California. Soft cover. *MCH&M.*

A History of Marine Attack Squadron 223. 1stLt Brett A. Jones, USMC. 1978. 39 pages. 19 photographs. 2 maps. Appendices. Details the activities of the "Bulldog" squadron from its first combat action at Guadalcanal through the Okinawa campaign of World War II, its years of training and readiness prior to its commitment to Vietnam action, and its postwar movements. Soft cover. *MCH&M.*

A History of Marine Fighter Attack Squadron 232. Maj William J. Sambito, USMC. 1978. 23 pages. 19 photographs. Appendices. Story of one of the oldest tactical squadrons in the Marine Corps; the "Red Devils" were activated in 1925 with field service in China, World War II, Vietnam, and Thailand. Soft cover. *MCH&M.*

A History of Marine Attack Squadron 311. Maj William J. Sambito, USMC. 1978. 67 pages. 35 photographs. 2 maps. Appendices. Narrative of the "Tomcat" squadron's actions in peacetime, World War II, Vietnam, and Thailand. Soft cover. *MCH&M.*

A History of Marine Fighter Attack Squadron 312. Maj William J. Sambito, USMC. 1978. 25 pages. 13 photographs. 2 maps. 1 diagram. Appendices. The famed "Checkerboard" squadron's exploits in World War II, Korea, and Vietnam are examined, as well as its peacetime training and deployments. Soft cover. *MCH&M.*

A History of Marine Fighter Attack Squadron 323. Col Gerald R. Pitzel, USMCR. 1987. 61 pages. 2 maps. 25 photographs. Appendices. 1943-1986. Exploits of the "Death Rattlers" on Okinawa, in Korea, and Vietnam. From Corsairs to Hornets. GPO 008-055-00173-1. $5.00. Soft cover. Available for library distribution.

Bibliographies

An Annotated Bibliography of the United States Marines in the Civil War. D. Michael O'Quinlivan and Rowland P. Gill. 1968. 15 pages. Deals with Marines on both sides in the war. Soft cover. *MCH&M.*

An Annotated Bibliography of the United States Marine Corps in the Second World War. D. Michael O'Quinlivan and Jack B. Hilliard. 1970. 42 pages. Index. Compilation of books dealing in whole or significant part with Marine Corps operations and related matters. Listings are general operations by geographical locations, post-hostilities operations, unit histories, biographies, and autobiographies. Soft cover. *MCH&M.*

An Annotated Bibliography of the United States Marine Corps in the Korean War. D. Michael O'Quinlivan and James S. Santelli. 1970. 32 pages. Index. Comprised of unclassified publications dealing in whole or in part with operations. Listings according to subject matter and, in the case of ground operations, according to geographical locations. Soft cover. *MCH&M.*

An Annotated Bibliography of the United States Marine Corps' Concept of Close Air Support. James S. Santelli. 1968. 24 pages. Listing of publications dealing in whole or in part with the development and employment of close air support within the Marine Corps. Period covered is first real combat employment of the technique through the Vietnam War. Soft cover. *MCH&M.*

An Annotated Bibliography of United States Marine Corps Artillery. Ralph W. Donnelly. 1970. 68 pages. Deals primarily with field artillery but includes material on antiaircraft defense and tactical rockets and missiles. Naval gunfire and ships' guns are not within the scope of this work. Brief section on manuscript material, considerable periodical references, and references to published photographs and training aids. Soft cover. *MCH&M.*

An Annotated Bibliography of Naval Gunfire Support. LtCol Harold A. Bivins, USMCR. 1971. 9 pages. Index. Listing of generally available articles and books that relate to naval gunfire support from its beginning through the war in Vietnam, including the recall of the battleship USS *New Jersey.* Soft cover. *MCH&M.*

Chronologies

A Chronology of the United States Marine Corps, 1935-1946, Volume II. Carolyn A. Tyson. 1971. 1977 reprint. 139 pages. Appendix. Marine Corps activities presented in time sequence and organized by geographic area. Covers introduction of amphibious concepts to the return to peacetime strength after World War II. Soft cover. *MCH&M.*

A Chronology of the United States Marine Corps, 1947-1964, Volume III. Ralph W. Donnelly, Gabrielle M. Neufeld, and Carolyn A. Tyson. 1971. 73 pages. Listing of Marine Corps activities by date and geographical location. Soft cover. *MCH&M.*

A Chronology of the United States Marine Corps, 1965-1969, Volume IV. Gabrielle M. Neufeld. 1971. 41 pages. Listing of Marine Corps activities by date and geographical locations. Derived from unclassified official records and suitable published contemporary works. Soft cover. *MCH&M.*

Catalogs

Marine Corps Oral History Collection Catalog. Benis M. Frank, compiler. 1974. 1979 rev. ed. 41 pages. Index. Summarizes subject matter covered in 192 oral history transcripts of interviews with retired distinguished Marines and other individuals with significant Marine Corps background. Soft cover. *MCH&M.*

Marine Corps Personal Papers Collection Catalog. Charles A. Wood, compiler. 1974. 1980 rev. ed. 56 pages. Index. Summarizes subjects and holdings of 163 manuscript collections and notes the availability of 55 unprocessed collections held by Marine Corps Historical Center. Soft cover. *MCH&M.*

Marine Corps Historical Publications Catalog: Available Publications List and Chronological Bibliography. Henry I. Shaw, Jr., compiler. 1988. 32 pages. In two parts, listing publications available from the Government Printing Offfice and the Marine Corps History and Museums Division with restrictions and all officially written or sponsored historical publications since 1920. Soft cover. *MCH&M.*

Registers of Personal Papers

Joseph Henry Pendleton, 1860-1942. Martin K. Gordon, compiler. 1975. 232 pages. 3 illustrations. Covers 66 years of Marine Corps history, especially the Philippines, Nicaragua, Dominican Republic, and Southern California. Soft cover. *MCH&M.*

George Barnett, 1859-1930. LtCol Merrill L. Bartlett, USMC, compiler. 1980. 18 pages. 1 photograph. Appendices. Principally the prewar and World War I papers of the 12th Commandant of the Marine Corps. Soft cover. *MCH&M.*

Clifton Bledsoe Cates, 1893-1970. Charles Anthony Wood, compiler. 1985. 36 pages. 1 photograph. Appendices. Index. Covers Cates' career from World War I to Commandant of the Marine Corps, 1948-51. Soft cover. *MCH&M.*

John H. Russell, Jr., 1872-1947. LtCol R. T. MacPherson, USMC (Ret), compiler. J. Michael Miller, editor. 1987. 58 pages. 1 photograph. Appendices. Index. Strongest in correspondence relating to Russell's tenure as High Commissioner in Haiti, as CMC 1934-36, and as a columnist for the *San Diego Union*, 1937-1946. Soft cover. *MCH&M.*

John Archer Lejeune, 1869-1942. LtCol Merrill L. Bartlett, USMC (Ret), compiler. 1988. 123 pages. 1 photograph. Covers some of the more than 6,600 documents of the Lejeune Papers in the Library of Congress, photocopied for the Marine Corps Historical Center, and a small collection of related items donated to the Center. Correspondence of the 13th Commandant is explored with particular reference to the nine years of his commandancy, which "remain the least known and appreciated of his accomplishments." Includes biographical sketch. Occasional paper. Soft cover. *MCH&M*.*

Special Publications

Guide to the Marine Corps Historical Center. 1987 rev. ed. 32 pages. 1 map. 13 photographs and illustrations. Describes the Center's location, physical plant, and facilities. Soft cover. *MCH&M.*

Marine Corps Historical Center Writing Guide. 1983 rev. ed. 74 pages. Contains chapters on research, writing, footnoting, bibliographies, map preparation, captioning, and indexing in Center style. Soft cover. *MCH&M*.

Finding Aid to Fortitudine, *Newsletter of the Marine Corps Historical Program. Volume II (1972-1973)-Volume XIII (1983-84)*. Richard A. Webster and Ian C. McNeal, compilers. 1984. 59 pages. Covers the quarterly's content in "Director's Page," articles, letters, and notices, "Oral History Report," "In Memoriam," and "World War II Chronology" categories. Soft cover. *MCH&M*.

Leadership Lessons and Remembrances from Vietnam. LtGen Herman Nickerson, Jr., USMC (Ret). 1988. 93 pp. Reproduction of a series of articles which appeared in *Sea Tiger*, the weekly newspaper distributed in the III Marine Amphibious Force area of northern South Vietnam, while Gen Nickerson was force commander (June 1969 - March 1970). Occasional Paper. Soft cover. *MCH&M*.

The Problems of U.S. Marine Corps Prisoners of War in Korea. James Angus MacDonald, Jr. 1988. 295 pp. A thesis prepared for a graduate-level degree in 1961 at the University of Maryland, this study has had a remarkable influence on official policies regarding prisoners of war since it was written. It is published for the use of the serious student of the POW experience. Occasional Paper. Soft cover. *MCH&M*.

To Wake Island and Beyond: Reminiscences. BGen Woodrow M. Kessler, USMC (Ret). 1988. 145 pages. Autobiographical account, in the author's highly readable script, of his experiences as a battery commander at Wake Island and as a Japanese POW. Occasional Paper. Soft cover. *MCH&M*.

Part II Marine Corps Historical Publications, 1920-1988

1920

The United States Marine Corps in the World War. Maj Edwin N. McClellan, USMC. 1920. 1968 reprint. 109 pp.

1925

History of the United States Marine Corps, 2 vols. Maj Edwin N. McClellan, USMC. 1925-1932. 2,274 pp.

1934

One Hundred Eighty Landings of the United States Marines, 1800-1934. Capt Harry A. Ellsworth, USMC. 1934. 1970 reprint. 163 pp.

1945

Guadalcanal Campaign, August 1942 to February 1943. 1945. 96 pp.

The Fifth Marine Division in World War II. 1stLt John C. Chapin, USMC. 1945. 26 pp.

The Fourth Marine Division in World War II. 1stLt John C. Chapin, USMC. 1945. 1976 reprint. 89 pp.

1946

Second Marine Division. John L. Zimmerman. 1946. 24 pp.

Campaign for the Marianas. 1946. 91 pp.

The Conquest of Okinawa: An Account of The Sixth Marine Division. Maj Philips D. Carleton, USMCR. 1946. 129 pp.

The Iwo Jima Operation. Capt Clifford P. Morehouse, USMCR. 1946. 174 pp.

The First Marine Division on Okinawa: 1 April-30 June 1945. Capt James R. Stockman, USMC. 1946. 79 pp.

The Sixth Marine Division. Capt James R. Stockman, USMC. 1946. 36 pp.

The First Marine Brigade (Provisional), Iceland. John L. Zimmerman. 1946. 18 pp.

1947

The Defense of Wake. LtCol Robert D. Heinl, Jr., USMC. 1947. 76 pp.

The Battle for Tarawa. Capt James R. Stockman, USMC. 1947. 86 pp.

1948

Marine Corps Traditions. 1948. 16 pp.

Marines at Midway. LtCol Robert D. Heinl, Jr., USMC. 1948. 56 pp.

Bougainville and the Northern Solomons. Maj John N. Rentz, USMCR. 1948. 166 pp.

1949

The Guadalcanal Campaign. Maj John L. Zimmerman, USMCR. 1949. 189 pp.

1950

Saipan: The Beginning of the End. Maj Carl W. Hoffman, USMC. 1950. 286 pp.

The Assault on Peleliu. Maj Frank O. Hough, USMCR. 1950. 209 pp.

Mobilization of the Marine Corps Reserve in the Korean Conflict. Capt Ernest H. Giusti, USMCR. 1950. 80 pp.

1951

Marine Aviation in the Philippines. Maj Charles W. Boggs, Jr., USMC. 1951. 166 pp.

The Seizure of Tinian, Maj Carl W. Hoffman, USMC. 1951. 169 pp.

1952

The Campaign on New Britain. LtCol Frank O. Hough, USMCR, and Maj John N. Rentz, USMCR. 1952. 186 pp.

1953

The Mobilization of the Marine Corps Reserve in the Korean Conflict. Capt Ernest H. Giusti, USMCR. 1953 revised edition. 1967 reprint. 60 pp.

1954

Iwo Jima: Amphibious Epic. LtCol Whitman S. Bartley, USMC. 1954. 253 pp.

The Marshalls: Increasing the Tempo. LtCol Robert D. Heinl, Jr., USMC, and LtCol John A. Crown, USMC. 1954. 188 pp.

The Recapture of Guam. Maj O. R. Lodge, USMC. 1954. 214 pp.

The Pusan Perimeter: U.S. Marine Operations in Korea, 1950-1953, vol. 1. Lynn Montross and Capt Nicholas A. Canzona, USMC. 1954. 271 pp.

1955

The Inchon-Seoul Operation: U.S. Marine Operations in Korea, 1950-1953, vol. 2. Lynn Montross and Capt Nicholas A. Canzona, USMC. 1955. 361 pp.

Okinawa: Victory in the Pacific. Maj Chas S. Nichols, Jr., USMC, and Henry I. Shaw, Jr. 1955. 332 pp.

1956

Marine Corps Ground Training in World War II. Kenneth W. Condit, Gerald Diamond, and Edwin T. Turnbladh. 1956. 353 pp.

1957

The Chosin Reservoir Campaign: U.S. Marine Operations in Korea, 1950-1953, vol. 3. Lynn Montross and Capt Nicholas A. Canzona, USMC. 1957. 432 pp.

1958

Pearl Harbor to Guadalcanal: History of U.S. Marine Corps Operations in World War II, vol. 1. LtCol Frank O. Hough, USMCR, Maj Verle E. Ludwig, USMC, and Henry I. Shaw, Jr. 1958. 439 pp.

A Brief History of the Marine Corps Base and Recruit Depot, San Diego, California. Elmore A. Champie. 1958. 22 pp.

A Brief History of the Marine Corps Base and Recruit Depot, Parris Island, South Carolina, 1891-1956. Elmore A. Champie. 1958. 27 pp.

A Brief History of Marine Corps Officer Procurement. Bernard C. Nalty. 1958. 36 pp.

The Diplomatic Mission to Abyssinia, 1903. Bernard C. Nalty. 1958. 39 pp.

The United States Marines in Nicaragua. Bernard C. Nalty. 1958. 39 pp.

1959

A Brief History of Certain Aspects of Manpower Utilization in the Marine Corps. Bernard C. Nalty. 1959. 12 pp.

The Barrier Forts: A Battle, A Monument, and A Mythical Marine. Bernard C. Nalty. 1959. 12 pp.

The Marines at Harpers Ferry, 1859. Bernard C. Nalty. 1959. 15 pp.

The United States Marines in the Civil War. Bernard C. Nalty. 1959. 16 pp.

The United States Marines in the War with Spain. Bernard C. Nalty. 1959. 1967 reprint. 20 pp.

The Lauchheimer Trophy. D. Michael O'Quinlivan. 1959. 10 pp.

1960

Hold High the Torch: A History of the 4th Marines. Kenneth W. Condit and Edwin T. Turnbladh. 1960. 458 pp.

A Brief History of the 1st Marines. Maj John H. Johnstone, USMC. 1960. 42 pp.

Inspection in the U.S. Marine Corps, 1775-1957. Bernard C. Nalty. 1960. 30 pp.

The Iwo Jima Flag Raising: The Event and the People. Bernard C. Nalty. 1960. 11 pp.

The United States Marines in North China, 1945-1949. Henry I. Shaw, Jr. 1960. 29 pp.

1961

The United States Marines in Iceland, 1941-1942. Maj Marvin L. Brown, Jr., USMCR. 1961. 17 pp.

A Brief History of the 3d Marines. Benis M. Frank. 1961. 32 pp.

A Brief History of the United States Marine Corps. Maj Norman W. Hicks, USMC. 1961. 52 pp.

Marine Corps Aircraft, 1913-1960. 1961. 18 pp.

Marine Corps Lore. 1961. 33 pp.

A Brief History of the 2d Marines. Maj John H. Johnstone, USMC. 1961. 21 pp.

United States Marine Corps Parachute Units. Maj John H. Johnstone, USMC. 1961. 21 pp.

A Chronology of the United States Marine Corps, 1775-1934.

Col William M. Miller, USMC, and Maj John H. Johnstone, USMC. 1961. 1965 reprint. 1970 reprint. 129 pp.

The United States Marines in the Gilberts Campaign. Bernard C. Nalty. 1961. 9 pp.

The United States Marines in the Marshalls Campaign. Bernard C. Nalty. 1961. 9 pp.

An Annotated Bibliography of the United States Marines in the Boxer Rebellion. D. Michael O'Quinlivan. 1961. 10 pp.

The United States Marines in the Guadalcanal Campaign. Henry I. Shaw, Jr. 1961. 1969 reprint. 14 pp.

The United States Marines in the Occupation of Japan. Henry I. Shaw, Jr. 1961. 1969 reprint. 34 pp.

A Brief History of the 9th Marines. Truman R. Strobridge. 1961. 27 pp.

A Brief History of Marine Corps Aviation. Elizabeth L. Tierney. 1961. 61 pp.

1962

The United States Marines in North China, 1945-1949. Henry I. Shaw, Jr. 1962 revised edition. 1968 reprint. 33 pp.

An Annotated Bibliography of the United States Marines in Guerilla-Type Action. Maj John H. Johnstone, USMC. 1962. 17 pp.

The East-Central Front: U.S. Marine Operations in Korea, 1950-1953, vol. 4. Lynn Montross, Maj Hubard D. Kuokka, USMC, and Maj Norman W. Hicks, USMC. 1962. 342 pp.

The United States Marines in the Battle for Iwo Jima. Bernard C. Nalty. 1962. 10 pp.

United States Marine Corps Ranks and Grades, 1775-1962. Bernard C. Nalty, Truman R. Strobridge, and Edwin T. Turnbladh. 1962. 45 pp.

An Annotated Bibliography of the United States Marines in the Korean War. D. Michael O'Quinlivan. 1962. 31 pp.

A History of Marine Corps Roles and Missions, 1775-1962. Col Thomas G. Roe, USMC, Maj Ernest H. Giusti, USMCR, Maj John H. Johnstone, USMC, and Benis M. Frank. 1962. 36 pp.

An Annotated Bibliography of the United States Marines in American Fiction. Truman R. Strobridge. 1962. 1964 reprint. 11 pp.

1963

Isolation of Rabaul: History of U.S. Marine Corps Operations in World War II, vol. 2. Henry I. Shaw, Jr. and Maj Douglas T. Kane, USMC. 1963. 632 pp.

A Brief History of Marine Corps Staff Organization. Kenneth W. Condit and Maj John H. Johnstone, USMC. 1963. 41 pp.

An Annotated Bibliography of the United States Marines in the Civil War. D. Michael O'Quinlivan. 1963. 11 pp.

A Brief History of the 5th Marines. Maj James M. Yingling, USMC. 1963. 66 pp.

1964

U.S. Marine Corps Monthly Calendar of Historical Events. Historical Branch, G-3 Division, HQMC. 1964. 102 pp.

Marine Corps Women's Reserve in World War II. Maj Pat Meid, USMCR. 1964. 99 pp.

1965

An Annotated Bibliography of the United States Marine Corps in the Second World War. D. Michael O'Quinlivan and Jack B. Hilliard. 1965. 42 pp.

A Chronology of the United States Marine Corps, 1935-1946. Carolyn A. Tyson. 1965. 1971 reprint. 1977 reprint. 139 pp.

1966

Marines in Lebanon, 1958. Jack Shulimson. 1966. 1983 reprint. 50 pp.

An Annotated Reading List of United States Marine Corps History. Jack B. Hilliard. 1966. 58 pp.

Central Pacific Drive: History of U.S. Marine Corps Operations in World War II, vol. 3. Henry I. Shaw, Jr., Bernard C. Nalty, and Edwin T. Turnbladh. 1966. 700 pp.

The United States Marines at Harpers Ferry and in the Civil War. Bernard C. Nalty. 1966 revised edition. 26 pp.

1967

The United States Marines on Iwo Jima: The Battle and the Flag-Raising. Bernard C. Nalty. 1967 revised edition. 1970 reprint. 29 pp.

Small Unit Action in Vietnam, Summer 1966. Capt Francis J. West, Jr., USMCR. 1967. 1977 reprint. 123 pp.

A Brief History of the 9th Marines. Truman R. Strobridge. 1967 revised edition. 30 pp.

An Annotated Bibliography of the United States Marine Corps in the First World War. Jack B. Hilliard. 1967. 16 pp.

1968

Victory and Occupation: U.S. Marine Corps Operations in World War II, vol. 5. Benis M. Frank and Henry I. Shaw, Jr. 1968. 945 pp.

Marine Corps Women's Reserve in World War II. LtCol Pat Meid, USMCR. 1968. 98 pp.

U.S. Marine Corps Civic Action Effort in Vietnam, March 1965-March 1966. Capt Russel H. Stolfi, USMCR. 1968. 96 pp.

A Brief History of the 1st Marines. Maj John H. Johnstone, USMC. 1968. 46 pp.

A Brief History of the 3d Marines. Benis M. Frank. 1968. 47 pp.

A Brief History of the 11th Marines. 2dLt Robert Emmet, USMCR. 1968. 58 pp.

An Annotated Bibliography of the United States Marines in the Civil War. D. Michael O'Quinlivan and Rowland P. Gill. 1968. 1983 reprint. 42 pp.

An Annotated Bibliography of the United States Marine Corps' Concept of Close Air Support. James S. Santelli. 1968. 24 pp.

Henry Clay Cochrane: Register of His Personal Papers. Capt Charles F. W. Coker, USMCR, compiler. 1968. 86 pp.

1969

The Battle for Khe Sanh. Capt Moyers S. Shore, USMC. 1969. 1977 reprint. 203 pp.

A Brief History of the 2d Marines. Capt Robert J. Kane, USMC. 1969. 58 pp.

1970

A Brief History of U.S. Marine Corps Officer Procurement. Bernard C. Nalty and LtCol Ralph F. Moody, USMC. 1970. 39 pp.

A Brief History of Headquarters Marine Corps Staff Organization. Kenneth W. Condit, Maj John H. Johnstone, USMC, and Ella W. Nargele. 1970. 49 pp.

United States Marine Corps Ranks and Grades, 1775-1969. Bernard C. Nalty, Truman R. Strobridge, Edwin T. Turnbladh, and Rowland P. Gill. 1970 revised edition. 62 pp.

The United States Marines in Iceland, 1941-1942. LtCol Kenneth J. Clifford, USMCR. 1970. 22 pp.

U.S. Marine Corps Civil Affairs in I Corps, Republic of South Vietnam, April 1966-April 1967. Capt William D. Parker, USMCR. 1970. 131 pp.

A Brief History of the 4th Marines. James S. Santelli. 1970. 68 pp.

An Annotated Bibliography of the United States Marine Corps in the Second World War. D. Michael O'Quinlivan and Jack B. Hilliard. 1970. 1982 reprint. 42 pp.

An Annotated Bibliography of the United States Marine Corps in the Korean War. D. Michael O'Quinlivan and James S. Santelli. 1970. 32 pp.

An Annotated Bibliography of United States Marine Corps Artillery. Ralph W. Donnelly. 1970. 68 pp.

Samuel Miller, 1814-1856: A Register of His Personal Papers. Doris S. Davis and Jack B. Hilliard, compilers. 1970. 50 pp.

McLane Tilton, 1861-1914: A Register of His Personal Papers. Charles A. Wood and Jack B. Hilliard, compilers. 1970. 45 pp.

1971

The Eagle, Globe, and Anchor, 1859-1969. Col John A. Driscoll, USMCR. 1971. 1977 reprint. 164 pp.

The Journal of Frank Keeler, 1898. Frank Keeler. Carolyn A. Tyson, editor. 1971. 50 pp.

An Annotated Reading List of United States Marine Corps History. Jack B. Hilliard and LtCol Harold A. Bivins, USMCR. 1971. 55 pp.

An Annotated Bibliography of Naval Gunfire Support. LtCol Harold A. Bivins, USMCR. 1971. 9 pp.

A Chronology of the United States Marine Corps, 1947-1964. Ralph W. Donnelly, Gabrielle M. Neufeld, and Carolyn A. Tyson. 1971. 73 pp.

A Chronology of the United States Marine Corps, 1965-1969. Gabrielle M. Neufeld. 1971. 41 pp.

Levi Twiggs, 1834-1850: A Register of His Personal Papers. Doris S. Davis, compiler. 1971. 28 pp.

John Lloyd Broome, 1849-1898: A Register of His Personal Papers. Doris S. Davis, compiler. 1971. 99 pp.

George C. Reid, 1898-1960: A Register of His Personal Papers. Doris S. Davis, compiler. 1971. 37 pp.

1972

United States Marine Corps Special Units in World War II. Charles L. Updegraph, Jr. 1972. 1977 reprint. 105 pp.

Operations in West Korea: U.S. Marine Operations in Korea, 1950-1953, vol. 5. LtCol Pat Meid, USMCR, and Maj James M. Yingling, USMC. 1972. 643 pp.

Western Pacific Operations—History of U.S. Marine Corps Operations in World War II, vol. 4. George W. Garnard and Truman R. Strobridge. 1972. 848 pp.

A Brief History of the 12th Marines. Charles R. Smith. 1972. 84 pp.

An Annotated Bibliography of Marines in the American Revolution. Carolyn A. Tyson and Rowland P. Gill. 1972. 76 pp.

Fortitudine: Newsletter of the Marine Corps Historical Program. 1971. Published quarterly to Spring 1987. Official newsletter of the History and Museums Division.

1973

Progress and Purpose: A Developmental History of the United States Marine Corps, 1900-1970. LtCol Kenneth J. Clifford, USMCR. 1973. 156 pp.

Louis McCarty Little, 1870-1960: A Register of His Personal Papers. Martin K. Gordon, compiler. 1973. 78 pp.

Wilburt Scott Brown, 1900-1968: A Register of His Personal Papers. Martin K. Gordon, compiler. 1973. 99 pp.

1974

Marines in the Dominican Republic, 1916-1924. Capt Stephen M. Fuller, USMCR, and Graham A. Cosmas. 1974. 109 pp.

Women Marines in World War I. Capt Linda L. Hewitt, USMCR. 1974. 65 pp.

Marine Flyer in France, The Diary of Captain Alfred A. Cunningham, November 1917-January 1918. Capt Alfred A. Cunningham, USMC. Graham A. Cosmas, editor. 1974. 43 pp.

The Marines in Vietnam, 1954-1973: An Anthology and Annotated Bibliography. 1974. 277 pp.

1st Marine Division and Its Regiments. 1974. 24 pp.

Marine Corps Oral History Collection Catalog. Benis M. Frank. 1974. 42 pp.

1975

Blacks in the Marine Corps. Henry I. Shaw, Jr., and Ralph W. Donnelly. 1975. 1988 reprint. 109 pp.

Marines in the Revolution: A History of the Continental Marines in the American Revolution, 1775-1783. Charles R. Smith. 1975. 500 pp.

Pictorial History of Marines in the Revolution. 1975. 32 pp.

Making a Continental Marine Uniform. Jack B. Hilliard and Doris S. Maley. 1975. 92 pp.

Civil War Marine: A Diary of the Red River Expedition, 1864. Frank L. Church. James P. Jones, and Edward F. Keuchel, editors. 1975. 89 pp.

3d Marine Division and Its Regiments. 1975. 25 pp.

Joseph Henry Pendleton, 1860-1942: A Register of His Personal Papers. Martin K. Gordon, compiler. 1975. 232 pp.

Marine Corps Oral History Collection Catalog. Benis M. Frank. 1975 revised edition. 41 pp.

Marines in the Revolution. Four-color plate series and descriptive pamphlet. Maj Charles H. Waterhouse, USMCR, artist, and Charles R. Smith. 14 plates and 32 pp. (Published by the Marine Corps Association)

1976

Marines and Helicopters, 1946-1962. LtCol Eugene W. Rawlins, USMC. Maj William J. Sambito, USMC, editor. 1976. 113 pp.

A Brief History of the 8th Marines. James S. Santelli. 1976. 103 pp.

1977

Marine Corps Aviation: The Early Years, 1912-1940. LtCol Edward C. Johnson, USMC. Graham A. Cosmas, editor. 1977. 107 pp.

U.S. Marines in Vietnam: The Advisory and Combat Assistance Era, 1954-1964. Capt Robert H. Whitlow, USMCR. 1977. 1982 reprint. 190 pp.

1978

A History of Marine Medium Helicopter Squadron 161. LtCol Gary W. Parker, USMC. 1978. 47 pp.

A History of Marine Attack Squadron 223. 1stLt Brett A. Jones, USMC. 1978. 39 pp.

A History of Marine Fighter Attack Squadron 232. Maj William J. Sambito, USMC. 1978. 23 pp.

A History of Marine Attack Squadron 311. Maj William J. Sambito, USMC. 1978. 67 pp.

A History of Marine Fighter Attack Squadron 312. Maj William J. Sambito, USMC. 1978. 25 pp.

Quantico: Crossroads of the Marine Corps. LtCol Charles A. Fleming, USMC, Capt Robin L. Austin, USMC, and Capt Chales A. Braley III, USMC. 1978. 146 pp.

U.S. Marines in Vietnam: The Landing and the Buildup, 1965. Jack Shulimson and Maj Charles M. Johnson, USMC. 1978. 260 pp.

Marines and Helicopters, 1962-1973. LtCol William R. Fails, USMC. 1978. 251 pp.

1979

Marine Corps Oral History Collection Catalog. Benis M. Frank. 1979 revised edition. 42 pp.

Guide to the Marine Corps Historical Center. 1979. 32 pp.

1980

Marine Corps Personal Papers Collection Catalog. Charles A. Wood. 1980. 56 pp.

George Barnett, 1959-1930: Register of His Personal Papers. LtCol Merrill L. Bartlett, USMC, compiler. 1980. 18 pp.

A Brief History of the 7th Marines. James S. Santelli. 1980. 83 pp.

1981

Marine Corps Historical Center Writing Guide. 1981. 63 pp.

A Brief History of the 25th Marines. Col Joseph B. Ruth, Jr., USMCR. 1981. 60 pp.

A Brief History of the 10th Marines. Maj David N. Buckner, USMC. 1981. 131 pp.

The 1st Marine Division and Its Regiments. 1981. 43 pp.

1982

The Colonel Robert D. Heinl, Jr., 1982 Memorial Award in Marine Corps History: Texts of the Winning Article and Those Receiving Honorable Mentions. 1982. 54 pp.

U.S. Marines in Vietnam: An Expanding War, 1966. Jack Shulimson. 1982. 390 pp.

A History of Marine Observation Squadron Six. LtCol Gary W. Parker, USMC and Maj Frank M. Batha, Jr., USMC. 1982. 71 pp.

A 'Do-It-Yourself' Oral History Primer. Benis M. Frank. 1982. 1985 reprint. 8 pp.

U.S. Marine Corps Marksmanship Badges from 1912 to the Present. Michael D. Visconage. 1982. 1983 reprint. 15 pp.

1983

Vietnam Historians Workshop: Plenary Session. Occasional Paper. 1983. 31 pp.

The Colonel Robert D. Heinl, Jr., 1983 Memorial Award in Marine Corps History: Texts of the Winning Article and Those Receiving Honorable Mentions. 1983. 42 pp.

Marine Corps Historical Center Writing Guide. 1983 revised edition. 74 pp.

U.S. Marine Corps Uniforms, 1983. Four-color plate series and descriptive pamphlet. Capt Donna J. Neary, USMCR, artist, and Capt Steven M. Berkowitz, USMC. 1983. 12 plates and 13 pp.

1984

Vietnam Revisited: Conversation with William D. Broyles, Jr. Col John G. Miller, USMC, editor. Occasional Paper. 1984. 48 pp.

Finding Aid to Fortitudine, Newsletter of the Marine Corps Historical Program, Volume II (1972-1973)-Volume XIII (1983-1984). Richard A. Webster and Ian C. McNeal, compilers. 1984. 59 pp.

U.S. Marines in Vietnam: Fighting the North Vietnamese, 1967. Maj Gary L. Telfer, USMC, LtCol Lane Rogers, USMC, and V. Keith Fleming, Jr. 1984. 338 pp.

1985

Chaplains with Marines in Vietnam, 1962-1971. Cdr Herbert L. Bergsma, CHC, USN. 1985. 240 pp.

The 2d Marine Division and Its Regiments. 1985. 56 pp.

The Marines in Vietnam, 1954-1973: An Anthology and Bibliography. 1985 revised edition. 373 pp.

Khe Sanh Bibliography. Occasional Paper. Ray W. Stubbe. 54 pp.

Marines in the Frigate Navy. Four-color plate series and descriptive pamphlet. Col Charles H. Waterhouse, USMCR, artist, and Charles R. Smith. 1985. 14 plates. 17 pp.

Clifton Bledsoe Cates, 1893-1970: Register of His Personal Papers. Charles Anthony Wood, compiler. 1985. 36 pp.

1986

U.S. Marines in Vietnam: Vietnamization and Redeployment, 1970-1971. Graham A. Cosmas and LtCol Terrence P. Murray, USMC. Maj William R. Melton, USMC, and Jack Shulimson, editors. 1986. 487 pp.

A History of the Women Marines, 1946-1977. Col Mary V. Stremlow, USMCR. 1986. 250 pp.

Alligators, Buffaloes, and Bushmasters: The History of the Development of the LVT Through World War II. Occasional Paper. Maj Alfred Dunlap Bailey, USMC (Ret). 1986. 272 pp.

75 Years of Marine Corps Aviation—A Tribute. An Exhibition of Art from the Marine Corps Museum. Benis M. Frank and John T. Dyer. 1986. 41 pp.

1987

Guide to the Marine Corps Historical Center. 1987 revised edition. 32 pp.

U.S. Marines in Grenada, 1983. LtCol Ronald H. Spector, USMCR. 1987. 35 pp.

A History of Marine Fighter Attack Squadron 323. Col Gerald R. Pitzel, USMCR. 1987. 61 pp.

U.S. Marines in Lebanon, 1982-1984. Benis M. Frank. 1987. 196 pp.

A Brief History of the 6th Marines. LtGen William K. Jones, USMC (Ret). 1987. 181 pp.

Fortitudine: Bulletin of the Marine Corps Historical Program. 1987. Published quarterly from Summer 1987 to date. Designated bulletin of the Marine Corps Historical Program.

1988

Leadership Lessons and Remembrances from Vietnam. LtGen Herman Nickerson, Jr., USMC (Ret). Occasional Paper. 1988. 93 pp.

The Problems of U.S. Marine Corps Prisoners of War in Korea. James Angus MacDonald, Jr. Occasional Paper. 1988. 289 pp.

John Archer Lejeune, 1869-1942: Register of his Personal Papers. LtCol Merrill L. Bartlett, USMC (Ret), compiler. Occasional Paper. 1988. 123 pp.

To Wake Island and Beyond: Reminiscences. BGen Woodrow M. Kessler, USMC (Ret). Occasional Paper. 1988. 145 pp.

Marine Corps Historical Publications Catalog: Available Publications List and Chronological Bibliography. Henry I. Shaw, Jr., compiler. 1988. 32 pp.